T0114759

The
DEVOTED MAN

A 5 Step Guide to take you from Dating App to Marriage

Derrick McQueen

WESTBOW
PRESS®
A DIVISION OF THOMAS NELSON
& ZONDERVAN

WestBow Press books may be ordered through booksellers or by contacting:

WestBow Press
A Division of Thomas Nelson & Zondervan
1663 Liberty Drive
Bloomington, IN 47403
www.westbowpress.com
844-714-3454

ISBN: 978-1-6642-6669-8 (sc)
ISBN: 978-1-6642-6668-1 (e)

Library of Congress Control Number: 2022909107

Print information available on the last page.

WestBow Press rev. date: 06/24/2022

Dedicated to my Wonderful Wife Mrs. Kali McQueen.

Dedicated to my Lovely Daughter Imani McQueen

Soli Deo Gloria

CONTENTS

PREFACE

Thank you for aligning yourself with the best ways to take you from single life to marriage. Moreover, this guide is to bridge that gap between frustration and your bride. This self-improvement manual offers a five-step guide for Christian men seeking to get married. It addresses many of the issues that come up in the dating process and presents single men with practical advice on approaching dating with the ultimate goal of marriage. Steps include working on yourself, creating a dating app profile, dating in person, getting engaged, and being married. Additionally, the text consists of scripture references throughout, which will help guide men toward the biblical principles that underpin the guide.

Let's talk about the definition of insanity for a moment. Insanity is where it all started for me. I thought the same things about dating for years, even though that approach wasn't working for me.

"Generally accepted wisdom is that the definition of insanity is doing the same thing repeatedly and expecting different results."

That being said, It's time to stop the headaches and build a great life, starting with a wonderful wife.

"Find a good spouse, you find a good life and even more: the favor of God" (Proverbs 18:22 MSG).

We will build. The biblical truths will be our boundaries and foundation, and on top of them, we will add on my helpful insights and experiences.

These spiritual truths will guard you against the ditches, mud, dirt, and sideshows of dating, saving you and the women you meet time, trouble, and heartache. To understand how these biblical principles operate, consider how the staff in a bowling alley might raise bumper rails for young and inexperienced bowlers to keep their balls from going into the gutter. The steps in this book should serve as bumper rails for you.

It's great that we can now be of the same intention as others looking strictly to find a spouse online. Make the beautiful dating app helpful, a tool.

Now, we agree that God knows what's best for us, right? Let's take a gander into God's design, his plan.

INTRODUCTION

I've always been interested in marriage, and I'm a believer. Now I'm even more of a believer. Why? In 2017, I decided to attempt to find my wife using not my understanding but God's ways. Where did I look? Where did I go to find her? A dating app. Dating apps were starting to get a more trustworthy reputation. I was frustrated with the looking-here-and-there approach, so I decided to focus on a dating app to find her, as it offered a way to date that would save me time but not shortcuts. The way I was dating previously was a waste of time. My behaviors during dating back then were casual and uncommitted at best, unfocused dead ends. Then my relationship with the Lord started to grow and I decided to date his way. The Red Sea parted.

So here we are. I decided to write this book to help and even coach men through their journey to marriage. Fellas, you may need some encouragement as you navigate the road of dating in the digital age, and that's OK.

As for me, I was a guy who always looked at the outside appearance of a woman. I gave it the most weight in evaluating that person for a potential relationship. The lady had to have a specific skin tone, height, and the right hair length. These were very shallow criteria, as you can discern. My old views were that if I could find a woman whose looks attracted me, I could work to change the inside stuff I didn't like. Another perspective I had was that sex had to be off the charts; the truth is we shouldn't have been having sex before marriage. I cringe as I recall those old views now. My actions came from the lust of the eyes and flesh. People in relationships on this level only use each other.

Magazines and videos filled my mind with how they wanted me to think about the opposite sex. I was caught in the culture of the world. I had it wrong. I was shackled, chained deep with others' perspectives. I was being filled, like a dumpster, with trash and not the truth.

So, where do we find this truth? We all need reality, and where better to get it than from the manufacturer of it all, our creator? Jesus is the way, the truth, and the life.

I had an earthly father, but he wasn't the type I could go to for advice. He was trying to get it right himself and survive. I never felt that I could go to him for life wisdom. He didn't live in the household and never married my mother. I didn't have a model of how a successful marriage should be or what made up healthy relationships. I didn't have principles or precepts to draw from or a successful couple to emulate growing up and into adulthood.

So, where do teens and young men in this situation get their learning? Their peers. The problem is that most of my friends had the same knowledge as me and came from the same brokenness.

I cringe again at all the misinformation passed along blindly, doing more damage than good through the years of friendship. The talk about the opposite sex and relationships was typical guy stuff—notches on your headboard, with no bona fide substance, not one ounce of godly wisdom anywhere to be found. I'm glad to say most of us eventually got it right, but there was so much time wasted, at least on my part.

So, where do we start to get the correct information? We gain knowledge and wisdom on dating from trusted sources—those who are in successful marriages. Then there is the first place to seek: our guide, Jesus. He is the light of the world. He is our moral compass. "I am the way, truth, and life; no one comes to the Father except through me" (John 14:6 AMP).

Slowly, by the grace of God and with his divine assistance, I became aware of the errors in my thinking. I could see clearly that my behaviors and thoughts toward women weren't true or righteous. They were selfish and not selfless. A change started to occur, and a shift began to happen in my consciousness. It didn't happen overnight, but I knew I was now on the right track.

Along the way, though, even when I thought I was ready, I wasn't. Few unsuccessful relationships brought heartache and lessons. Learning from my mistakes and wrong approaches led me to my wife.

What is the one thing that causes the most problems in dating and relationships before marriage? Sex. It can complicate every area of your life outside of marriage. Why? First, sex clouds your perceptions and blinds you to the essential character traits of your partner. Second, sex before the wedding takes you further away from your goal of marriage rather than closer.

Quick sidebar on one of the clues dropped by my wonderful wife that showed me she might be the one. We were not together in person but planning a camping trip on the phone. At this point in my journey, I had already made a vow of abstinence until marriage, and my future wife said as we were planning the trip camping that she would come up to the campsite for the day, but she would not spend the night. *Ding, ding, ding!* Could she also be on the journey of abstaining from sex until marriage and living by the higher principles?

In the text ahead, each step will be a guide on your journey to wedlock, offering a helpful list of dos and don'ts that will serve as your guidelines. The measures present practical wisdom to keep you in the game of dating the right way, the righteous path.

1

S T E P

WORK ON YOURSELF FIRST

What Do You Have to Bring to the Table?

Husbands, go all out in your love for your wives, exactly as Christ did for the church—a love marked by giving, not getting. Christ's love makes the church whole. His words evoke her beauty. Everything he does and says is designed to bring the best out of her, dressing her in dazzling white silk, radiant with holiness. And that is how husbands ought to love their wives.

They're doing themselves a favor since they're already one in marriage (Ephesians 5:25–28).

"The major key to your better future is you."
—Jim Rohn's quote taken from

https://www.success.com/rohn-the-major-key-to-your-best-future-is-you/

The first step is to work on yourself. Become aware of yourself, your soul, inner life, thoughts, and actions. Are your current thoughts and actions giving you your best life? If they are not, change them. The goal is to become the master of yourself and your mind. All you have in you (the Spirit of Truth, the Word of God, God, and Jesus) is greater than the devil in the world. Abide in Jesus, and he will live in you.

First, identify your strengths and weaknesses. Work to strengthen your powers. Strive to eradicate your liabilities, such as addictions, procrastination, inner self-criticism, and the tendency to be distracted. This work on yourself will make you the best version of yourself, not only for yourself but for those connected to you, like your future bride.

Sit down and reflect. Write down the areas in your life you need to work on that would make you a fantastic husband. What areas in your life need to heal or transform? Before we go to step 2, ask yourself: What positives do I bring to a relationship? What do I genuinely have to give? What are my beliefs, truths, goals, assets, visions for the future, and support system? Keep answers to these questions at the forefront of your mind going forward. They will give you intentionality, boldness, and direction. Your due diligence in this area will pay off handsomely down the road.

"Be ye not unequally yoked together with unbelievers, for what fellowship does righteousness have with unrighteousness? What communion does light have with darkness?" (2 Corinthians 6:14 JUB).

On working on yourself, I will share a game changer with you. It's God's way, I obeyed it, and I was able to experience spiritual perspective, purity, and a host of other benefits.

Abstinence. Prepare yourself to abstain from sex altogether until marriage. This one change in behavior and thinking will clear the way to discover the best wife for you. Abstinence will also get you to your wedding day sooner rather than later. How? You'll avoid so many pitfalls and distractions without sex. Momentary pleasure can be devastating. Sex opens up a host of potential problems, attachments, emotions, and unnecessary feelings that will take you off the path to life. We don't want that as devoted men. You will gain clarity of thinking by abstaining, and your goal will be to get to know the character of your dates, not their flesh.

Share your commitment to abstinence with your dates early on in the dating process. Your dates' response to your dedication will give you insight into their values and where they are on their journey. For example, they may respond by saying they believe in sex before marriage, or they believe in sex on the first date. As you know, what business does light have with darkness? Your old self might have said, "Well, I'm all in with that." Not now. You're on an intentional path. You don't want that.

On the other hand, your date may be willing to abstain and open to learning God's way regarding dating. As for me, I purchased a simple engraved bracelet from Amazon for little money that stated "Abstinence until Marriage" to remind me daily of my vow to be celibate. It gave me unexpected strength and support. Also, a Proverbs 31 woman would appreciate you abstaining from sex for yourself and your future bride. Just think of finding the one and telling her you had remained pure for her before you even met.

Sex is a gift that is not to be enjoyed outside the confines of marriage. As the pastor who married my wife and me stated in premarital counseling, sex is great. It's like a fire. Used correctly, as in a fireplace, it gives heat and warmth to the whole house. But it can burn down that house if used outside the fireplace. When you overcome that instant gratification monster, your life becomes laser-focused. So take sex off the table. Get an accountability partner or wise friend to help you stay strong if needed.

> For this is the will of God, that you be sanctified [separated and set apart from sin]: that you abstain and back away from sexual immorality; that each of you knows how to control his own body in holiness and honor [being available for God's purpose and separated from things profane], not [to be used] in lustful passion, like the Gentiles who do not know God and are ignorant of His will, and that [in this matter of sexual misconduct] no man shall transgress and defraud his

brother because the Lord is the avenger in all these things, just as we have told you before and solemnly warned you. For God has not called us to impurity, but to holiness [to be dedicated and set apart by behavior that pleases Him, whether in public or in private]. So whoever rejects and disregards this is not [merely] rejecting man but the God who gives His Holy Spirit to you [to dwell in you and empower you to overcome temptation]. (1 Thessalonians 4:3–8 AMP)

While you are working on yourself, keep the following in mind:

- Don't hide health issues. Prepare yourself; be honest and transparent.
- Be aware by being honest with yourself about problems in specific areas of your life. For instance, do you have

any addictions to porn, drugs, impulse shopping, gluttony, or greed?

- Don't seek or get the average guy feedback or encouragement. Be aware of bad advice from friends. Seek wise counsel.
- Don't hide your parenting situation. Do you have children?
- If you have in-home children, don't expect to treat your children better than your future wife's children (if she has children). Know what you are getting into.
- Do be over your ex-girlfriends or ex-wives before you start to date. It's only fair to your dates and yourself.
- Do be aware of your financial situation. Are you in debt? If so, how much? Are you working on a plan to get you out of debt?
- Make a list of the things you have to bring to the table.
- Think about whether you would relocate for someone.

- Do seek and take advice from seasoned married couples. They have gems to give, lessons learned, and wisdom to share. My favorite question to a seemingly happy married couple is, "What's the secret?"
- What will your wife look like? What will be the contents of her character? "Charm can mislead and beauty soon fades. The woman to be admired and praised is the woman who lives in the Fear-of-God" (Proverbs 31:30–31 MSG).
- Do seek help to break addictions.

You got this! Reach out to me if you need an accountability partner, coaching, or help to obtain sources in breaking addictions. I will include an email address toward the end of the book for you to reach me.

"We do not enjoy being disciplined. It is painful at the time, but later, after we have learned from it, we have peace because we start living the right way" (Hebrews 12:11 NCV).

2
STEP

CREATE YOUR DATING APP PROFILE

First off, I know some less-than-desirable dating sites, but let me recommend Match.com and Eharmony.com. These are good sites for the devoted man. I met my wife on Match.com.

"Here's another way to put it: You're here to be light, bringing out the God-colors in the world. God is not a secret to be kept. We're going public with this as a city on a hill. If I make you light-bearers, you don't think I'm going to hide you under a bucket, do you? I'm putting you on a light stand-shine! Keep an open house; be generous with your lives. By opening up to others, you'll prompt people to open up with God, this generous Father in heaven" (Matthew 5:14–16 MSG).

Now is the time! You've worked on yourself, and you have a realistic view of your bride plus more self-awareness. Let's go for it!

The goal of creating a profile is to stand out with substance, truth, sincerity, and authenticity. Be humble.

An essential part of your profile will be your profile pictures. Make your lead photo one that is straight on, with no clutter in the background. Hiring a freelance photographer to take a headshot of you wouldn't be a bad investment for the devoted man. Have three to four profile pictures, but be intentional about each one. Each photo should illustrate something about you. Put your best foot forward. A great photo draws a woman in. You want it to affect her so that she thinks. I *have to click on this profile and know more about this guy.* Remember, you want to attract the woman you will spend the rest of your life with.

It's also crucial that you somehow state that you are a believer if you are a believer. Think "evenly yoked." Be creative.

Before dating, make a list of your must-have qualities and values in a woman: height, weight, race, kids, income, and location. What things can you do without compromising?

Hold on to faith that the right woman will appreciate all the work you are doing for her good. Of course, after your profile is up and running, reach out to profiles of women you find interesting.

"The reward of humility [that is having a realistic view of one's importance] and the [reverent, worshipful fear of the Lord is riches, honor, and life" (Proverbs 22:4 AMP).

See also Proverbs 3:34 and James 4:6.

Pray and believe in yourself, your intentions, and what you offer. Know you are doing your best and putting great action in front of great choices. Pray constantly.

- Keep your profile clean and straightforward. Don't use profile pictures with bare pecs or your kids in them. You want a Proverbs 31 woman to take you seriously.
- Don't go overboard with your bio, saying too much. Be intentional and concise.
- Don't just look at the physical appearance of women when browsing profiles.
- Do state your intentions.
- Be sincere, and do not play games or lead a woman on whom you discern may not be the one for you.

- Add joy to your profile; smile in your profile picture at least once.
- Do be patient; the proper connection may not happen overnight.

3
S T E P

DATING IN PERSON

Congratulations! Now you've found someone you're interested in and who seems interested in you. Way to go! Keep your eyes on the big picture, the end goal—marriage. Date correctly, stay pure and don't be blinded by her beauty.

"As a ring of gold in a swine's snout So is a beautiful woman who is without discretion [her lack of character mocks her beauty]" (Proverbs 11:22 AMP).

Stay deliberate on dates. Let your true self shine, relax, and be intentional. Stay away from pointless conversations. Focus; you can't get back your time.

Sensitivity toward your dates will minimize hurt feelings should things not work out. You should see your date as another human being who deserves the same treatment you desire. Spared feelings are a benefit of ethical dating.

If things do not work out, an unspoken level of respect will permeate the end of dating. You were intentionally on the up and up and in the open about everything. You didn't take advantage of her. Plus, your conscience will be clear.

Stay as positive as possible. Dating is and should be an exciting time. Allow this guide to serve as your bowling alley bumper rails. Follow the principles; they will keep you moving down the road to marriage without going into the proverbial gutter.

- Don't kiss until you are dating seriously, and depending on your self-control, hold off on that entirely. Of course, you should be attracted to your potential wife, but kissing can lead to other things.
- Don't enter her home or vice versa as you continue to date. Stay pure. Temptation is all around.
- Do be gentle with your words. "Words kill, words give life; they're either poison or fruit—you choose" (Proverbs 18:21 MSG).
- Do let her go if you're not interested; don't waste her time so she can be free to find her Boaz.
- Meet in public places such as coffee shops, restaurants, and parks.
- Do ask questions to get to know her and feel whether you would be evenly yoked.
- Do smile.
- Do give a brief hug or handshake— nothing over the top.
- Do possess a warm presence.

- Do be fully present; put your cell phone away.
- Do open doors.
- Do pay attention to whether your dates keep their word, are honest, and are on time.
- Do pay for the first date, coffee, or meal.
- Do show compassion when she shares something real about her life, health, finances, family, etc. Be empathetic! Don't be insensitive.

4
STEP

GETTING ENGAGED

Let me share the eternal truth of love with you—
what it is and what it is not. Look through the
lens of this definition while moving forward.

> Love endures with patience
> and serenity, love is kind and
> thoughtful and is not jealous or
> envious; love does not brag and
> is not proud or arrogant. It is not
> rude; it is not self-seeking, it is not
> provoked [nor overly sensitive and
> easily angered]; it does not take

into account a wrong endured. It does not rejoice at injustice but rejoices with the truth [when right and truth prevail]. Love bears all things [regardless of what comes], believes all things [looking for the best in each one], and hopes all things [remaining steadfast in difficult times] [without weakening]. Love never fails [it never fades or ends]. (1 Corinthians 13:4–8 AMP)

You've found the one—nicely done! This is an exciting time in your life, and the decision to go all the way is final. Enjoy this time, and make the proposal about her. Make it unique and memorable. If her parents, close siblings, or extended family are around, call them and tell them your plans. It's not so much asking their permission as it is including them.

Get creative and authentic with your proposal, and make it make sense to you. Videotape it, or have someone take plenty of pictures. Whatever resonates with you both as a couple is fair to include.

After she says yes, the planning begins. I would strongly recommend premarital counseling from at least one source if not two. Perspectives from both male and female counselors would be ideal. Make sure they are accredited, and if they are believers, you're on the right track.

> "Refuse good advice and watch your plans fail; take good counsel and watch them succeed" (Proverbs 15:22 MSG).

One of the benefits of counselors is that they will be able to point out blind spots that you may not be able to see in your fiancée and vice versa. Another is that they will ask the tough questions that are maybe hard to ask on your own when you both are one on one. Lastly, a good counselor is an objective third party.

If you are following this guide, you two haven't lived together yet, so counseling will give you insight and confidence moving forward into the marriage.

- Do still abstain from sex.
- Do be flexible with wedding plans.
- Do plan for moving after the wedding— who, where, how, and when.
- Do continue to pray.
- Do take your dating profile down.
- Do embrace the wise counsel you receive.

5

S T E P

MARRIAGE

You did it the right way; I'm sincerely happy for you. To God be the glory! Ephesians 5:25–33 AMP

Mark 10:5–9 MSG

Communication is vital and valuable. Don't hesitate to continue with counseling or go back as needed.

God willing, you will be blessed with many prosperous years together. One of my premarital counselors said—or as his wife said to him during early rough patches in their marriage—"We're stuck; you're not going anywhere." That's the attitude you want. It will not be sunny every day, but marriage will be the gift that keeps on giving on most days.

Be quick to listen, give plenty of mercy, forgive, and don't keep a tally of wrongs. If something goes wrong, work it out! You're one flesh now, and the best is yet to come.

- Don't neglect the small things. Loving her is loving yourself because the two are now one. Encouraging her and building her up daily will nourish her and benefit you.
- Seek out and engage with successfully married couples—mature couples who have been at this for some time. Take their advice, and apply their wisdom to your situations.
- Do keep counseling in place.
- Do keep lines of communication open.

- Do be mindful of the truth that you are the head of the household. And as our female counselor pointed out, the marriage should look like a dance where you know the man's leading, but you can't tell because the couple moves together so well.
- Don't take for granted that you are the head of the household. Be sensitive to the woman as the weaker sex.
- Do plan date nights together.
- Have weekly or monthly budget meetings to plan the management of finances.
- Leave anger way in the back.
- Delight in this journey together.

"The very steps we take come from God otherwise how would we know where we're going?" (Proverbs 20:24)

Thanks for reading. Let me know how it's going for you and what step you're on! Email me at Derrick@Dundating.com if you would like one-on-one coaching or a dating app review.

Recommended Books Kingdom Man, by Tony Evans

The Wait, by Devon Franklin and Megan Good

Financial Peace, by Dave Ramsey

Follow me on Medium: @derrickmcqueen

Follow me on Twitter: @DerrickMcQueen

ABOUT THE AUTHOR

 Derrick McQueen is a mature Christian who, through experience backed up by Biblical principles, gained clarity on the dating process. This clarity will help get you to the point of a healthy marriage. To boot, McQueen met his wife online.

Visit me at my internet home
DerrickMcQueen.co